Th
A JU
JUNGLY JOKES
belongs to

Ronald Mannion.

Also available in Beaver by John Hegarty

A VERY MICE JOKE BOOK
NOT THE ELEPHANT JOKE BOOK

A JUMBLE OF JUNGLY JOKES

John Hegarty

Illustrated by Mike Gordon

Beaver Books

A Beaver Book
Published by Arrow Books Limited
62–5 Chandos Place, London WC2N 4NW

An imprint of Century Hutchinson Ltd

London Melbourne Sydney Auckland
Johannesburg and agencies throughout the world

First published 1988

Set in Century Schoolbook
by JH Graphics Ltd, Reading

Made and printed in Great Britain
by Anchor Brendon Ltd
Tiptree, Essex

ISBN 0 09 953250 6

For Louise and Catherine

Contents

Introduction

What did the cannibal say to the jungle explorer?
'Doctor Livingstone, I consume!'

What's big, blue and wrinkled?
An elephant holding its breath.

What were Tarzan's last words?
'Who greased that vine?!'

Welcome, Explorers, to the darkest and steamiest, wildest and woolliest joke book ever! Soon you'll be wading waist-deep through snappy crocodile jokes, hacking your way through highly dangerous banana jokes . . . Discover every known species of wild humour, from aardvark jokes to zebra jokes . . . Have a shot at some big game hunter jokes, devour whole pages of cannibal jokes . . .

You'll laugh like a hyena, howl like a monkey, at **A Jumble of Jungly Jokes** – the world's first ever jungle joke safari. So on with your pith helmet, and let's get cracking . . .

An army of ant jokes

What is smaller than an ant's mouth?
What the ant eats.

What do you call a stupid ant?
Ignorant.

PASSENGER IN PLANE: Look at all those people
down there – they look just like ants.
HER HUSBAND: *They are ants, you fool – we
haven't taken off yet.*

Two ants were running as fast as they could
across the top of a box of cornflakes. 'Hey!'
puffed one ant, 'what are we running so fast
for?' 'Can't you read?' said the other. 'It says:
Tear along the dotted line.'

How many insects are needed to fill a building?
Tenants!

TEACHER: Let us think about the busy ant. He
works all the time, night and day. Then
what happens?
SMART ALEC: *Someone treads on him.*

What do you call a young male ant that floats?
Buoyant.

What is an antelope?
When two ants run away to get married.

What is the definition of romance?
Two Italian ants in love.

What did the Pink Panther say when he trod on the ant?
(Sing 'Pink Panther' tune) 'Dead-ant, dead-ant, dead-ant-dead-ant-dead-ant . . .'

What do ants take when they are ill?
Antibiotics.

What is the smallest ant in the world?
An infant.

How do you get an ant out of your ear?
Pour chocolate down it and it will come out a Treet.

What are the biggest ants in the world?
Giants.

What do you call a group of ants that takes the law into its own hands?
Vigilantes.

What do you call an old ant?
An antique.

Where is the coldest place ants can live?
The Antarctic.

What do you get if you cross an ant with a block of ice?
Antifreeze.

Why did the ant dance on top of the jam jar?
Because it said 'Twist to open'.

What is a foreign ant?
Important.

What is the definition of an ant?
An insect that works hard but still finds time to go to all the picnics.

What did the bee say to the ant?
'Your honey or your life.'

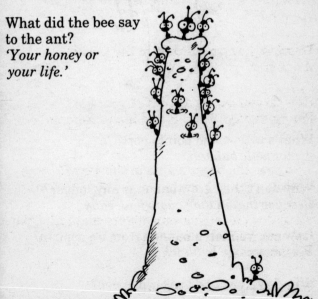

A bunch of banana jokes

Why don't bananas have dandruff?
Did you ever see a banana with hair?

What's yellow and points north?
A magnetic banana.

Why don't they grow bananas any longer?
Because they're long enough already.

How can you tell a banana from an aspirin?
Bananas come in bunches.

What's yellow and goes beep-beep?
A banana in a traffic jam.

What's yellow, washable, dries quickly and needs no ironing?
A drip-dry banana.

Why don't bananas care what people say about them?
Because they're thick-skinned.

What's yellow and goes click-click?
A ball-point banana.

What's yellow and flickers?
A banana with a loose connection.

What's yellow on the inside and green on the outside?
A banana disguised as a cucumber.

What's yellow and plays football?
Banana United.

A buzz-load of bee jokes

Where do bees wait for transport?
At a buzz-stop.

'Waiter, waiter, there's a
bee in my soup.'
*'Yes sir, it's alphabet
soup.'*

Why is a bee-hive like a rotten potato?
A bee-hive is a bee-holder, and a bee-holder is a spectator, and a specked tater is a rotten potato.

Why is hunting for honey like a legacy?
Because it is a bee-quest.

What's a bee?
An insect that stings for its supper.

What's furry, stings, collects nectar, and is hard to understand?
A mumble bee.

What's brown and yellow and flies along the bottom of the ocean?
A bee in a submarine.

Knock, knock.
Who's there?
Abbey.
Abbey who?
Abbey stung me on the nose.

What do you get if you cross a pub with a line of bees?
A barbecue (bar-bee-queue).

What do you get if you cross a bee with a bell?
A humdinger.

CUSTOMER: Waiter, there's a bee in my soup.
WAITER: *Yes sir, it's the fly's day off.*

What's the most intelligent insect you'll ever meet at school?
A spelling bee.

What do bees say in summer?
'Swarm.'

'Doctor, doctor, I've been stung by a bee.'
'Shall I put some cream on it?'
'Don't be silly, it'll be miles away by now!'

What is worse than being with a fool?
Fooling with a bee.

Why do bees hum?
Because they don't know the words.

What do you get if you cross a bee and a skunk?
Something that stings and stinks at the same time.

What do you get if you cross a bee with half a pound of mince?
A humburger.

What did the bee say to the flower?
'Hello, honey.'

What do you call a bee born in May?
A maybe.

What are the bees on strike for?
More honey and shorter flowers.

What do bees do with honey?
They cell it.

What goes zzub, zzub?
A bee flying backwards.

Why do bees have sticky hair?
Because they have honey combs.

What animal is really stupid and hums?
A wally-bee.

A flock of bird jokes

What do you call a woodpecker with no beak?
A headbanger.

Knock, knock.
Who's there?
Toucan.
Toucan who?
Toucan live as cheaply as one.

Which bird likes to eat sawdust?
A woodpecker.

What lives in the jungle trees and is highly dangerous?
A toucan with a machine gun.

What do you get if you cross a sweet with a bird?
A fudgerigar.

What do you do with sick budgies?
Have them tweeted.

What bird can't sing?
A humming bird.

What is the strongest bird in the world?
A crane.

NEWS ITEM: Pelicans are so expensive to feed, that zookeepers are now faced with very large bills.

Did you hear about the idiot who took a packet of budgie seed back to the pet shop and complained? He told the shopkeeper that he had planted the seeds but no budgies had grown.

TEACHER: Why do birds fly south in winter?
DUMBO PUPIL: *'Cos they can't swim, Miss.*

What succeeds?
A toothless budgie!

'Quick!' said the panic-stricken man in the pub,
'does a lemon have legs?'
　'No, of course not,' came the reply.
　'Oh no! That means I've just squeezed the
canary into my gin . . .'

What bird will never have a vote in an
election?
A mynah bird, because he's under 18.

'My budgie lays square eggs.'
'Gosh! Can it talk as well?'
'Yes, but it only says one word.'
'What's that?'
'Aaarrrgggh!'

1ST MAN: I've come to help you move your piano.
2ND MAN: *Thanks, but I've got it upstairs already.*
1ST MAN: All by yourself?
2ND MAN: *No, I hitched the budgie to it.*
1ST MAN: But how on earth could a tiny budgie drag a grand piano up two flights of stairs?
2ND MAN: *Easy – I used a whip.*

A big catch of big cat jokes

ALEX: If you were surrounded by six lions, six tigers, six leopards and six pumas, how would you get away from them?

TIM: *I'd wait for the merry-go-round to stop and then I'd get off!*

Why is it dangerous to play cards in the jungle?
Because there are so many cheetahs about.

Did you hear about the tiger who caught measles?
He became so spotty he was sent to a leopard colony.

What's the definition of a panther?
Someone who makes panths!

Why are leopards spotted?
So you can tell them from fleas.

LION TO BIG CAT: You're a dreadful cheetah!
CHEETAH: *You're no better — you're always lion!*

Did you hear about the idiot who bought his wife a jaguar?
It bit her and ran away.

What's the fastest member of the cat family?
An E-type Jaguar!

Knock, knock.
Who's there?
Jaguar.
Jaguar who?
Jaguar nimble, jaguar quick . . .

A cauldron of cannibal jokes

What kind of person is fed up with people?
A cannibal.

What do cannibals play at parties?
Swallow my leader.

Why should you always remain calm when you
meet a cannibal?
Well, it's no good getting in a stew, is it?

WAITER ON SHIP: Would you like to see the
  menu sir?
CANNIBAL: *No, just bring me the passenger list.*

Why did the cannibal go to the wedding
reception?
So that he could toast the bride.

1ST CANNIBAL: I don't know what to make of
  my husband these days.
2ND CANNIBAL: *How about a nice casserole?*

1ST CANNIBAL: Am I late for dinner?
2ND CANNIBAL: *Yes, everyone's eaten.*

1ST CANNIBAL: I don't think much of your wife.
2ND CANNIBAL: *Never mind, just eat the
  vegetables instead.*

CANNIBAL: How much do you charge for dinner here?

WAITER: *£2 a head, sir.*

CANNIBAL: Well, I'll have a couple of legs too, please.

A cannibal mother and her son were watching a big airliner fly across the sky. 'What's that?' asked the boy.

'Well, it's a bit like a lobster,' said the mother. 'You only eat the inside.'

What does the vegetarian cannibal eat?
Swedes.

A creep of crawly jokes

What has 50 legs but can't walk?
Half a centipede.

Two caterpillars were sitting on a jungle plant when a butterfly flew by. One caterpillar said to the other caterpillar: 'They'll never get me up in one of those things!'

What do you call a guard with 100 legs?
A sentrypede.

What is a caterpillar?
A worm in a fur coat.

What's green and highly dangerous?
A caterpillar with a hand-grenade.

What did one caterpillar say to the other
caterpillar when a lady centipede walked past?
*'What a lovely pair of legs, pair of legs, pair of
legs . . .'*

What goes 99-plonk, 99-plonk?
A centipede with a wooden leg.

PLONK!

What's green, hairy and turns into a 5 ton
truck?
A caterpillar tractor.

NASTY BOY TO FATHER: 'Dad, how many legs
   do you have to pull off a millipede before it
   limps?'

A crunch of crocodile jokes

Why is a camera like a crocodile?
Because they both snap.

DICK: Would you prefer that a crocodile ate
 you, or a tiger?
CHRIS: *I'd prefer that the crocodile ate the tiger!*

What's worse than a crocodile with tooth-ache?
A centipede with bunions.

What do you get if you cross a maths teacher
with a crocodile?
Snappy answers.

Knock, knock.
Who's there?
Althea.
Althea who?
Althea later, alligator!

MAN ON SAFARI: I'd love to swim in that river,
 but there might be crocodiles in there.
SAFARI GUIDE: *No, there aren't any crocodiles.*
MAN ON SAFARI: How do you know?
SAFARI GUIDE: *Because the piranha fish have
 chased them all away.*

If a crocodile makes shoes, what does a banana make?
Slippers!

'Waiter, bring me a crocodile sandwich, and make it snappy . . .'

WOMAN IN SHOE SHOP: Can I have a pair of crocodile shoes, please?
SHOP ASSISTANT: *Certainly, madam. What size does your crocodile take?*

'Would you wear crocodile shoes?'
'No, I never wear second-hand clothes.'

Why are crocodiles easy to fool?
Because they swallow anything.

A woman tourist was admiring a Red Indian's necklace. 'What are those stones around your neck?' she asked.

'Not stones,' the Indian replied. 'Alligator teeth.'

'Gosh,' said the woman. 'I suppose they hold the same meaning for you as pearls do for us.'

'Not quite,' came the reply. 'Anybody can open an oyster . . .'

What's the difference between a crocodile and a sandwich?
A sandwich doesn't bite your legs off.

A trampling of elephant jokes

Why do elephants wear sandals?
To stop their feet sinking in the sand.

Why do ostriches bury their heads in the sand?
To see the elephants who aren't wearing sandals.

What do you get if you cross an elephant with a bad motorist?
A trunk'n' driver.

How do you stop an elephant from passing through the eye of a needle?
Tie a knot in his tail.

Why do elephants have cracks between their toes?
So that they can hold their bus tickets.

DICK: What's the difference between an elephant baby and a matterbaby?
MICK: *What's a matterbaby?*
DICK: Nothing, what's wrong with you?

What do you get if you cross an elephant with the abominable snowman?
A jumbo yeti.

Why do elephants have wrinkled feet?
To give the ants half a chance.

What did the elephant say into the microphone?
'Tusking, tusking . . . one, two, three, tusking . . .'

What transport do elephants use?
Ele-copters.

Why does an elephant wear plimsolls?
To sneak up on mice.

A croak of frog jokes

What ballet is most popular with frogs?
Swamp Lake.

What is green and spins around at 100mph?
A frog in à liquidizer.

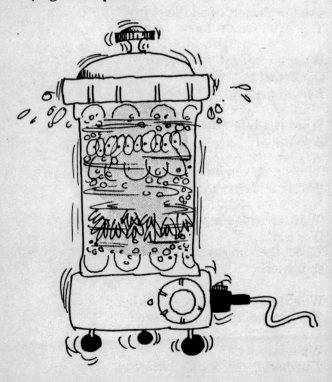

What do you call a girl with a frog on her head?
Lily.

Did you hear about the unlucky princess who kissed a handsome prince and he turned into a frog?

What do you get if you cross a galaxy with a toad?
Star Warts.

'Doctor, doctor, I feel like a frog!'
'Can't you see I'm busy – hop it.'

What do you get if you cross a muppet with a thick mist?
Kermit the Fog.

What is a frog's favourite sweet?
A lollihop.

'Waiter, do you have frogs' legs?'
'No sir, I always walk like this.'

'Waiter, do you have frogs' legs?'
'Yes sir.'
'Good, then hop over the counter and get me a sandwich.'

What happened to the frog when it died?
The poor thing simply croaked.

What is a cloak?
The mating call of a Chinese frog.

What goes dot-dot-croak, croak-dot-dot, croak-croak-dot?
Morse toad.

What do frogs drink?
Croaka Cola.

A chicken went into the library and said, 'Buk, buk,' so the librarian gave it a book. The chicken left the library, went to sit by a pond, and said, 'Buk, buk.' A frog suddenly appeared from the water and said, 'Reddit, reddit!'

What do you call a frog spy?
A croak and dagger agent.

How do frogs die?
They Kermit suicide.

What's the weakest animal in the world?
A frog. He will croak if you touch him.

Where do frogs leave their hats and coats?
In the croakroom.

A safari of hunter jokes

1ST BIG GAME HUNTER: We may as well give up – we haven't hit a single tiger all day.

2ND BIG GAME HUNTER: *Let's miss a couple more and then we'll go home.*

What did the leopard say after he'd eaten the hunter?
That sure hit the spot!

PUSS, PUSS, PUSS, PUSS

What is a big game hunter?
A chap who loses his way to a first division football match.

BOASTING HUNTER: '. . . so I just leapt out of my camp-bed, grabbed my gun, and shot the tiger in my pyjamas.'

CLEVER DICK: *'Goodness me, what was a tiger doing in your pyjamas?'*

SAFARI GUIDE: Quick sir, shoot that leopard on the spot!

IDIOT HUNTER: *Be specific, you fool — which spot?*

The safari guide came running out of the jungle, into the game hunter's tent. 'I've just spotted a leopard,' he shouted.

'You can't fool me,' replied the hunter. 'They're born that way.'

What did one lion say to the other lion when they saw the hunter in his Land Rover?
'Oh look, meals on wheels.'

When a hunter put his head into the lion's mouth to see how many teeth it had, what did the lion do?
It closed its mouth to see how many heads the hunter had.

A big game hunter failed to return to his camp one night. Said one of his fellow hunters: 'He must have disagreed with something that ate him.'

PHHT!

1ST LION: That hunter who camped near the lake last night has been eaten.
2ND LION: *How do you know?*
1ST LION: I've got inside information.

MOTHER LION: What are you doing, son?
BABY LION: *I'm chasing a hunter around a tree.*
MOTHER LION: How many times must I tell you not to play with your food?

41

A gangle of giraffe jokes

What is the highest form of animal life?
The giraffe.

Giraffes are so tall, they have to stand on a chair to brush their teeth.

ERIC: Why do giraffes have long necks?
BILL: *Because their feet smell?*
ERIC: No, to connect their heads to their bodies.

What is Dracula's favourite animal?
The giraffe — just think of all that neck!

TEACHER: Name ten animals from Africa.
PUPIL: *Nine elephants and a giraffe.*

Do you know why giraffes are nosey?
Because they're always looking over walls to see what giraffe-ter (you're after).

What do you get if you cross a giraffe with a hedgehog?
A twenty foot toothbrush.

What do you get if you cross a giraffe with a dog?
An animal that barks at low-flying aircraft.

Which animal takes the longest time to apologize?
The giraffe – it takes him a long time to swallow his pride.

What's worse than a giraffe with a sore throat?
A tortoise with claustrophobia.

What is writing on the wall of a zoo called?
Giraffiti.

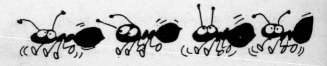

A gang of gorilla jokes

What do you get if you cross a gorilla with an angry dog?
Very nervous postmen!

What do you get if you cross a gorilla with an idiot?
A chumpanzee.

What is big and hairy and flies at Mach 2?
King Kongcorde.

Why do gorillas scratch themselves?
Because they're the only ones who know where they itch.

What's the difference between a biscuit and a gorilla?
Ever tried dunking a gorilla?

Why did King Kong climb Cleopatra's Needle?
To get his kite.

Where does a gorilla sleep?
Anywhere it wants to.

Why did the gorilla lie in the middle of the path?
To trip up the ants.

What would you get if you crossed a gorilla
with a bell?
A ding-dong King Kong.

Who rings the bell twice then knocks down the
door?
The Avon gorilla.

JANE: I can trace my ancestry all the way back
    to royalty.
JILL: *King Kong?*

Why did King Kong join the army?
He wanted to study gorilla warfare.

What's big and hairy and climbs up the Empire
State Building in a dress?
Queen Kong.

Why don't gorillas eat penguins?
Because they can't get the wrappers off.

What do you call a gorilla who works as a car mechanic?
A grease monkey.

What do you call a gorilla with two bananas in his ears?
Anything you like, because he can't hear you.

GORILLA: Doctor, my hair keeps falling out. What can you give me to keep it in?
DOCTOR: *Try this cardboard box.*

GORILLA: Doctor, I don't know what's the matter with me. I've gone right off bananas and spend all day dreaming about apples.
DOCTOR: *Cor!*

Knock, knock.
Who's there?
Gorilla.
Gorilla who?
Gorilla cheese sandwich for me and I'll be right over.

A policeman stopped a man who was walking along with a gorilla and ordered him to take it to the zoo at once. The next day the policeman saw the same man, still with the gorilla. 'I thought I told you to take that gorilla to the zoo,' he said. 'I did,' said the man, 'and now I'm taking him to the pictures.'

FRED: Did I ever tell you about the time I came face to face with a very fierce gorilla?
BERT: *No, what happened?*
FRED: Well, I stood there, without a gun . . . The gorilla looked at me and snarled and roared and beat his chest. Then it came closer and closer . . .
BERT: *What did you do?*
FRED: Oh, I'd had enough, so I moved on to the next cage.

A hotch-potch of hippo jokes

How do you make a hippo fly?
Start with a 6ft zip.

Why do hippos wear glasses?
So that they don't bump into other hippos.

What's grey, spotty, and weighs two tons?
A hippo with measles.

What do you get if you cross a space pistol, a cheer, and a hippopotamus?
A hip-hippo-ray gun!

What do hippopotamuses have that no other animals have?
Baby hippos.

1ST HIPPO: What's that thing over there?
2ND HIPPO: *That's a rhinoceros.*
1ST HIPPO: Fancy having to go through life with a face as ugly as that!

What weighs over a ton and wears flowers in its hair?
A hippy potamus.

What's the biggest species of mouse in the world?
The hippopotamouse.

What do you give to a seasick hippopotamus?
Lots of room.

What's grey and fat and goes up the front of anoraks?
A zipperpotamus.

An inferno of insect jokes

Did you hear about the idiot who chased the daddy long legs around for hours until he realized he had a crack in his glasses?

Who is top of the insect charts?
Bug's Fizz.

What do you get if you cross a bug with the Union Jack?
A patrio-tick.

What do insects learn at school?
Mothematics.

What is green, sooty and lives in the grass rubbing its legs together?
Chimney cricket.

What has tiny wings and is related to the camel?
A hump-backed midge.

What makes the letter T so important to a stick insect?
Without it, it would be a sick insect.

How do termites relax?
They take a coffee table break.

SID: Where do all the jungle bugs go in winter?
JOE: *Search me.*
SID: No thanks, I just wanted to know.

What's the best way to prevent infection from
biting jungle insects?
Don't bite any.

On which ship did the first insects sail to
America?
The Mayflower.

What do you call an insect from outer space?
Bug Rogers.

What did the earwig sing at the football
match?
'Earwigo, earwigo, earwigo . . .'

A pride of lion jokes

DEBBIE: I just saw a lion with spots.
FIONA: *You mean a leopard.*
DEBBIE: No, it was a lion with measles.

Why does a lion have a fur coat?
Because he would look daft in a plastic mac.

Why were the Colosseum managers in ancient Rome angry with their lions?
Because they were eating up all their prophets (profits).

What do you call a vain lion?
A dandy lion.

Why is a lion in the desert like Christmas?
Because of his sandy claws.

What must a lion tamer know to teach a lion tricks?
More than the lion.

What lion can't roar?
A dandelion.

What will a lion eat in a restaurant?
The waiter.

Why do lions eat raw meat?
Because they don't know how to cook.

What steps should you take if you see a mad lion?
Very, very big ones!

What is the difference between a wet day and a lion with toothache?
One is pouring with rain, the other is roaring with pain.

What is the most important part of a lion?
The mane part.

DICK: Where did you get that beautiful stuffed lion?
BERT: *In Africa — I went on a big game safari with my uncle Fred.*
DICK: What's he stuffed with?
BERT: *My uncle Fred.*

Why are missionaries popular with man-eating lions?
Because they go down very well.

1ST LION: Every time I eat a missionary, I'm sick.
2ND LION: *That's because you can't keep a good man down.*

Why couldn't the telephone caller get through
to the zoo?
Because the lion was out of order.

What do you do when you see a big fierce lion?
Hope he doesn't see you.

A lady was taking her son around the museum
when they came across a huge stuffed lion in a
glass case. 'Mum,' asked the puzzled boy, 'how
did they shoot the lion without breaking the
glass?'

What drink does the king of the jungle like
best?
Lyons Quick Brew.

What is the equator?
An imaginary lion running round the earth.

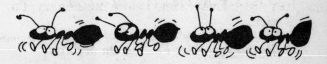

A mix-up of motley jokes

Knock, knock.
Who's there?
Aardvark.
Aardvark who?
Aardvark a million miles, for one of your
smiles . . .

What's the wasps' favourite TV channel?
The Bee-Bee-C.

Just before a cricket match:
GRAEME: How do you hold a bat?
ALISTAIR: *By the wings, of course!*

What does a bat sing in the rain?
'Raindrops Keep Falling On My Feet.'

RICK: Do aardvarks go on safari?
GILL: *Not safaris I know.*

JOHN: A man was walking through the jungle
and a pintcost came out and bit him.
JENNY: *What's a pintcost?*
JOHN: About 90p.

What do you get if you cross an alligator with
an iceberg?
A cold snap.

What do you get if you cross a hyena with a
mynah bird?
An animal that laughs at its own jokes.

What's grey, has sharp teeth and holds up
socks?
An alligarter.

How can you make a sloth fast?
Take away its food.

A mish-mash of motley jokes

Did you hear about the short-sighted turtle?
It fell in love with a crash helmet.

What do you get if you cross a hyena with an
Oxo cube?
A laughing stock.

CUSTOMER: Can I have some rat poison,
    please?
CHEMIST: *Have you tried Boots?*
CUSTOMER: I want to poison them, not kick
    them to death!

DEBBIE: I have a canary that can do something
    I can't.
EMMA: *What's that?*
DEBBIE: Take a bath in a teacup.

Knock, knock.
Who's there?
Anteater.
Anteater who?
Anteater whole jar of jam.

What's a termite's favourite breakfast?
Oak meal.

Knock, knock.
Who's there?
Iguana.
Iguana who?
Iguana hold your hand.

Knock, knock.
Who's there?
Gnu.
Gnu who?
Gnu lamps for old!

A howling
of monkey jokes

Knock, knock..
Who's there?
Bab.
Bab who?
Bab Boone is a real ape.

Knock, knock.
Who's there?
Beryl.
Beryl who?
Beryl load of monkeys.

What does the government use when it takes a
census of all the monkeys in the zoo?
An ape recorder!

How do monkeys know the date?
They eat it.

What's the definition of guerilla warfare?
Monkeys throwing coconuts at each other!

'Is that your own face, or are you breaking it in
for a baboon?'

How do monkeys keep rumours circulating?
On the apevine.

**What is the difference between a monkey, a
bald man and the Prince of Wales?**
*A monkey is a hairy parent, a bald man has no
hair apparent, and the Prince of Wales is the
heir apparent.*

Knock, knock.
Who's there?
Monkey.
Monkey who?
Monkey won't fit, that's why I'm knocking.

Knock, knock.
Who's there?
Willoughby.
Willoughby who?
Willoughby a monkey's uncle!

What's yellow and smells of bananas?
Monkey sick.

What's green and swings through the trees?
A septic monkey.

What keys are furry?
Monkeys.

What do you get if you cross a monkey with a Scottish dance and a joker?
An ape-reel fool.

How do you catch a monkey?
Hang upside down from a tree and make a noise like a banana.

GARY: I was thrown out of the zoo last week for feeding the monkeys.
RICHARD: *What's so bad about that?*
GARY: I was feeding them to the lions.

ALEX: Mummy, is it true that we're descended from apes?
MOTHER: *I don't know. I never met your father's family.*

HELP!

Why is a monkey like a flower?
Because it's a chimp-pansy.

How do monkeys toast bread in the jungle?
They put it under the g'riller!

What swings through trees and is very dangerous?
A monkey with a machine-gun.

What's a monkey that eats chips called?
A chip monk.

TEACHER: If you saw me standing by a
monkey, what fruit would it remind you of?
PUPIL: *A pear.*

A buzz-load of mosquito jokes

Knock, knock.
Who's there?
Amos.
Amos who?
Amosquito bit me.

Knock, knock.
Who's there?
Ann.
Ann who?
Another mosquito.

'My wife is so cold-blooded, when mosquitoes bite her, they die of pneumonia.'

What is a mosquito with the itch?
A jitterbug.

What goes dit-da-dit-dit-da-dit-bzzzzzz and then bites you?
A morsequito.

Two mosquitoes were having a chat on Robinson Crusoe's back. One said to the other, 'I've got to go now, but I'll see you on Friday.'

What's the difference between a man bitten by a mosquito and a man going on holiday?
One is going to itch: the other is itching to go.

A well-travelled explorer was talking about the huge mosquitoes of the African jungle. 'Are they vicious?' asked one of the audience.
   'No,' the explorer replied casually, 'they'd eat out of your hand.'

Why could mosquitoes be called religious?
First they sing over you, then they prey on you.

A flutter of moth and butterfly jokes

RICK: What kind of fly can you spread on toast?
DAVE: *I didn't think there was any fly you could spread on toast!*
RICK: Oh yes . . . a butterfly!

What's the biggest moth ever known?
The mammoth.

What comes out of a wardrobe at a hundred miles an hour?
Stirling Moth.

What do you get if you cross a butterfly with a Russian naval commander?
A Red Admiral.

What is a myth?
A lady moth that hasn't got married.

MAN: These mothballs you sold me are no good.
SHOPKEEPER: *Why not?*
MAN: I haven't hit a single moth yet.

Why did the moth nibble a hole in the carpet?
Because he wanted to see the floor show.

What is pretty, has big teeth and flies?
A killer butterfly.

A pandemonium of panda jokes

What is black and white and found in the desert?
A lost panda.

What do you get if you cross a panda with a harmonium?
Pandamonium.

What is black and white and has eight wheels?
A panda on roller skates.

What do you call a bald panda?
Fred Bear.

What do you get if you cross a panda bear with
a harp?
A bear-faced lyre.

What's red and white and full of policemen?
A sunburnt Panda.

Why was the policeman crying?
*Because he couldn't take his Panda to bed with
him.*

Why do panda bears have fur coats?
They'd look silly in tweed ones!

What do you get if you cross a panda with a
kangaroo?
A fur coat with pockets.

What have Chi-Chi the Panda and Winnie the
Pooh got in common?
Their middle name.

A chatter of parrot jokes

MAN IN PET SHOP: A packet of Persil please, to wash my parrot.

SHOPKEEPER: *If you wash your parrot in Persil you'll kill it.*

MAN: I'll take a chance.

(3 days later)

SHOPKEEPER: Ah, how's the parrot?

MAN: *It's dead.*

SHOPKEEPER: I told you that washing it in Persil would kill it.

MAN: *Oh no, it wasn't the Persil – it was the spindryer that did it.*

PARROT: Us parrots are smarter than you chickens.

CHICKEN: *Oh yeah? And what makes you say that?*

PARROT: Ever seen Kentucky Fried Parrot?

COALMAN TO HOUSEWIFE: Your parrot's a good talker.

PARROT: *I can count, too – put in another bag!*

Knock, knock.
Who's there?
Parrot.
Parrot who?
It's a-Parrot you don't want to see me.

What do you get if you cross a parrot with a soldier?
A parrot-trooper.

Why can't you find aspirins in the jungle?
Because the parrots eat 'em all (paracetamol)!

Did you hear about the man who bought his mother a very rare parrot for her birthday? It could speak ten languages, play chess, and sing the entire works of Mozart. He asked her what she thought of the bird. 'It was delicious, son,' she said, 'absolutely delicious . . .'

GARY: Why do you keep your parrot's cage over the stove?

RICHARD: *It feels at home on the range.*

LITTLE BOY TO PARROT IN ZOO: Say, little birdie, can you talk?

PARROT: *Yes — can you fly?*

What do you get if you cross a parrot with a homing pigeon?

A bird that asks its way home if it gets lost.

TEACHER: What is a polygon?

THICK PUPIL: *An empty parrot cage, Miss.*

What singing birds come from Cornwall?
The Parrots of Penzance.

'Doctor, doctor, I feel like a parrot.'
'Just perch there a minute.'

TEACHER: Why do we put a hyphen in bird-cage?
PUPIL: *For the parrot to perch on.*

BOY TO PET SHOP OWNER: Can I have some
    parrot seed, please?
PET SHOP OWNER: *Oh, you've got a parrot, have
    you?*
BOY: No, but I'd like to grow one.

What do you get if you cross a parrot with a
centipede?
A walkie-talkie.

JIM: I once had a parrot for five years and it
    never said a word.
SID: *That's unusual. Why do you think that
    was?*
JIM: It was stuffed.

What do you get if you cross a parrot with a
woodpecker?
*A bird that knocks on doors and delivers
messages.*

A scientist has successfully crossed a hyena
with a parrot. Now he knows what hyenas
laugh at.

Did you hear about the scientist who crossed a parrot with a crocodile?
It bit off his arm and said, 'Who's a pretty boy then?'

WHO'S A PRETTY BOY?

What game do parrots enjoy?
Monopolly.

What did the cheeky parrot say to the ugly parrot?
'With a face like that, you'd better learn to say something other than "Pretty Polly!"'

Where do parrots go to study?
A polly technic.

ANGRY CUSTOMER: That parrot you sold me won't say a word, and you promised it would repeat everything it heard!
PET SHOP OWNER: *So it will, sir – only it's stone deaf.*

A prickle of porcupine jokes

What pine has the sharpest needles?
A porcupine.

What's green and prickly?
A seasick porcupine.

Did you hear about the idiot porcupine?
He fell in love with a scrubbing brush.

How do porcupines cuddle each other?
With great care.

What is a prickly pear?
Two porcupines.

What did the baby porcupine say when he
backed into a cactus?
'Is that you, ma?'

In the fight between the porcupine and the
lion, who won?
The porcupine won on points.

What did the Daddy porcupine say to his son as
he was about to spank him?
*'This is going to hurt me a lot more than it
hurts you . . .'*

What is the favourite food of porcupines?
Prickled onions.

A rumbling of rhinoceros jokes

ADAM: And I shall call that creature over there a rhinoceros.
EVE: *But why call it that?*
ADAM: Because it looks like a rhinoceros, stupid!

If milk comes from a cow, where does wine come from?
From a wine-oceros.

TEACHER: What family does the rhinoceros belong to?
PUPIL: *I don't know, Miss, nobody in our street has one.*

How do you stop a rhino charging?
Take away its credit card.

What's huge and wrinkled and jumps every two seconds?
A rhino with hiccoughs.

DICK: Did you know that rhinoceroses eat with their tails?
BERT: *You're joking!*
DICK: No I'm not – they sleep with them, too.

Which rhino is a Hollywood star?
Rhino Neal.

TEACHER: Can you tell me one of the uses of
  rhino skin?
PUPIL: *Yes, it keeps the rhino together.*

What's huge and wrinkled, and bounces?
A rhino on a pogo stick.

A whiff of skunk jokes

JANE: Why are you crying?
JACK: *Nobody likes me. Even my pet skunk wears a gas mask.*

TEACHER: Do we get fur from skunks?
PUPIL: *Yes, we get just as fur as we can!*

What did the judge say when he saw the skunk in the courtroom?
'Odour in court!'

What do you get if you cross an owl with a skunk?
A bird that smells but doesn't give a hoot.

How many skunks do you need to make a big stink?
Just a phew.

How do you stop a skunk from smelling?
Hold his nose.

Why did the skunk need an aspirin?
Because he had a stinking headache.

LOUISE: How is a skunk different from a tiger?
ANNE: *I don't know. How?*
LOUISE: The skunk uses a cheaper deodorant!

What do you get if you cross a skunk with a porcupine?
A porcupong.

BABY SKUNK: Can I have a chemistry set?
MOTHER SKUNK: *No, it makes the house smell.*

Why do skunks argue?
Because they like to raise a stink.

What is black and white and red behind?
A skunk with nappy rash.

A slug of slimy jokes

'Waiter, I've just found a slug in my salad!'
'Well, *that's better than finding half a slug,
isn't it?*'

'Waiter, waiter, I've had an accident with the
salad.'
'*What seems to be the trouble, sir?*'
'My knife slipped and I cut this slug in half.'

'Doctor, doctor, I feel like a snail.'
'Mmm, you need to be brought out of your shell.'

BOY: I was eating some salad, and I swallowed a slug.
DOCTOR: *Goodness! Let me give you something for it.*
BOY: No thanks – I'll just let it starve.

What makes a glow-worm glow?
It eats light meals.

Where do you find giant snails?
On the end of giants' fingers.

Why is the snail one of the strongest creatures in the jungle?
Because it carries its house on its back.

What do you get if you cross Dracula with a snail?
The world's slowest vampire.

Did you hear about the stupid woodworm?
It was found in a brick!

TEACHER: Can anyone tell me what sort of
   animal a slug is?
PUPIL: *Yes, sir — a snail with a housing
   problem.*

Knock, knock.
Who's there?
Weevil.
Weevil who?
Weevil only be staying a minute.

A slither of snake jokes

What is a viper's favourite food?
Hiss fingers!

What's long and green and goes 'hith'?
A snake with a lisp.

What do you do with a green snake?
Wait until it ripens.

Which hand would you use to grab a poisonous snake?
Your enemy's.

Why did the two boa constrictors get married?
Because they had a crush on each other.

What is a snake's favourite opera?
Wriggletto.

What do you do if you cross a snake with a government employee?
A civil serpent.

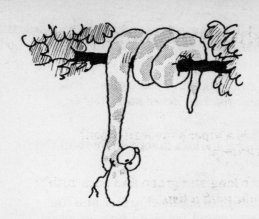

What do you get if you cross an snake with a
Lego set?
A boa constructor.

What do you do if you cross a glow-worm with a
python?
A twenty-foot strip-light.

What do you get if you cross an adder with a
trumpet?
A snake in the brass.

What do you get if you cross a snake with a
magic spell?
Addercadabra . . . or Abradacobra.

What happened to the snake with a cold?
She adder viper nose.

Then there was the Egyptian snake dancer
who couldn't tell her asp from her elbow.

A little boy saw a grass snake for the first time. 'Mother,' he cried, 'here's a tail without a body!'

Why can't you play jokes on snakes?
Because you can never pull their legs.

What is a snake's favourite football team?
Slitherpool.

What did the snake-charmer and the undertaker get for wedding presents?
Two towels marked 'Hiss' and 'Hearse'.

1ST JUNGLE BOY: Look, there's a baby snake.
2ND JUNGLE BOY: *How do you know it's a baby?*
1ST JUNGLE BOY: I can tell by its rattle.

What kind of snake likes pastry?
A pie-thon, of course!

What happened when a deadly rattlesnake bit JR?
It died in agony.

TOURIST: Is it true that the snakes in the jungle will not harm you if you carry a copy of **A Jumble of Jungly Jokes?**
SAFARI GUIDE: *Depends how fast you carry it.*

What is a snake's favourite sweet?
Wriggley's chewing gum.

'Quick, doctor, I've been bitten by a snake. I've only a few seconds to live.'
'Right, I'll be with you in a minute.'

What do you get if you cross a wild pig with a snake?
A boar constrictor.

A shudder of spider jokes

What's black and hairy and goes up and
down?
A spider in a lift.

Knock, knock.
Who's there?
Webster.
Webster who?
Webster Spin,
the spider.

CUSTOMER: Waiter, there's a spider in my
   soup.
WAITER: *That'll be twenty pence extra.*

What do you call an Irish spider?
Paddy Longlegs.

What's a spider's favourite television
programme?
The Newly-Web Game.

CUSTOMER: Waiter, there's a spider in my
   soup. Send me the manager.
WAITER: *That's no good, sir, he's frightened of
   them too.*

What did Mrs Spider say when Mr Spider
broke her new web?
'Darn it!'

What did the spider say to the beetle?
'Stop bugging me.'

What are spiders' webs good for?
Spiders.

TEACHER: What did Robert the Bruce do after
   watching the spider climbing up and down?
PUPIL: *He went and invented the yo-yo.*

A treeful of Tarzan jokes

What did Tarzan say when the tiger started chewing his leg?
'AAAAAAAAAAARRRRRRRRRGGGGG-HHHHHHHH!' (Give Tarzan yell)

What's purple and swings through the trees?
Tarzan of the Grapes.

What's yellow, tastes of almonds and swings from cake to cake?
Tarzipan.

What were Tarzan's dying words?
'Who greased that vine?'

What did Tarzan say when he saw the elephants coming?
'Here come the elephants.'

Where does Tarzan get his clothes?
At a jungle sale.

What does Tarzan sing at Christmas?
'Jungle bells, Jungle bells . . .'

What is the jungle animals' national anthem?
Tarzan Stripes Forever.

Who is Tarzan's favourite singer?
Harry Elephante.

An attack of tiger jokes

How can you get a set of teeth put in for free?
Smack a tiger.

What do you get if you cross a plum with a
tiger?
A purple people-eater.

There was a young man from the city,
Who met what he thought was a kitty;
He gave it a pat,
And said, 'Nice little cat!'
They buried his clothes, what a pity.

What's the best way to talk to a man-eating tiger?
By long-distance telephone.

JANE: Who went into a lion's den and came out alive?
JACK: *Daniel.*
JANE: Who went into a tiger's den and came out alive?
JACK: *I don't know.*
JANE: The tiger!

'Have you ever seen a man-eating tiger?'
'No, but I once saw a man eating chicken.'

GARY: My Dad faced a fierce tiger in the jungle and didn't turn a hair.
DICK: *I'm not surprised — your Dad's bald!*

DORIS: I hear you've just come back from India?
DUDLEY: *That's right — I was the guest of a rajah.*
DORIS: Did you go hunting?
DUDLEY: *Oh yes. One day we went into the jungle to shoot tigers.*
DORIS: Any luck?
DUDLEY: *Yes — we didn't meet any!*

There was a young lady from Riga,
Who rode with a smile on a tiger.
They returned from the ride
With the lady inside,
And the smile on the face of the tiger.

A zoo-load of zebra jokes

What do you get if you cross a zebra with an ape-man?
Tarzan stripes for ever.

What's black and white and lives at the North Pole?
A lost zebra.